POTTER V. SHRACKLE

AND

THE SHRACKLE CONSTRUCTION COMPANY

Seventh Edition

Deposition File
Defendant Materials

D1605225

POTTER V. SHRACKLE

AND

THE SHRACKLE CONSTRUCTION COMPANY

Seventh Edition

Deposition File
Defendant Materials

Kenneth S. Broun

Henry Brandis Professor of Law Emeritus
University of North Carolina School of Law

Frank D. Rothschild
Attorney at Law
Kilauea, Hawaii

Revision by Kenneth S. Broun and Frank D. Rothschild based upon the original file
created by Kenneth S. Broun as revised by James H. Seckinger

THE NATIONAL INSTITUTE FOR TRIAL ADVOCACY

Address inquiries to:
Reprint Permission
National Institute for Trial Advocacy
1685 38th Street, Suite 200
Boulder, CO 80301-2735
Phone: (800) 225-6482
Fax: (720) 890-7069
Email: permissions@nita.org

ISBN 978-1-60156-747-5
FBA 1747
eISBN 978-1-60156-752-9
FBA 1752

Printed in the United States of America

Official co-publisher of NITA.
WKLegaledu.com/NITA

CONTENTS

ACKNOWLEDGMENTS

The authors would like to thank the following for their assistance in the creation of the photographs and video clips that come with this file: Craig Gilbert, general contractor (Charles Shrackle); Bobby Dudley, former contractor and now Kona lawyer (Jeffrey Potter); Bob Bissenette, commercial painter (James Marshall); Courtney Haas, realtor and yoga instructor (Cheryl Tobias); and especially Anne Slifkin, attorney and mediator, whose portrayal of Kathy Potter in the original version of this file (c. 1976) became part of NITA lore.

We are also deeply indebted to Juan Gonzalez III, Principal, and Jaime Jue, Senior Associate, in the forensic department of KPMG LLP for their outstanding work in upgrading and enriching the experts portion of this file, including the reports and tables of Dr. Glenn and Dr. Buchanan, the Dyer memorandum, and other related materials.

INTRODUCTION

This is a wrongful death action brought in Nita State Court by Jeffrey T. Potter, as administrator of the estate of his deceased wife, Katherine, and in his own behalf, against Charles T. Shrackle and the Shrackle Construction Company. Potter claims that Shrackle negligently drove the company's pickup, striking Katherine Potter as she was crossing the street, causing her death. Potter claims that Shrackle was acting in the course of the Shrackle Construction Company's business at the time of the accident.

Shrackle admits striking Ms. Potter, but claims that she was crossing in the middle of the street, rather than in the pedestrian crosswalk, and that she did not look before entering the street in the path of Mr. Shrackle's truck. Defendants deny that Shrackle was negligent and allege contributory negligence on the part of the deceased, Ms. Potter.

Electronic versions of all exhibits and the PowerPoint presentation are available for download at http://bit.ly/1P20Jea; the password is Potter7D.

IN THE CIRCUIT COURT OF
DARROW COUNTY, NITA
CIVIL DIVISION

Jeffrey T. Potter, the	)	
Administrator of the Estate	)	
of Katherine Potter, and	)	
Jeffrey T. Potter, individually,	)	
	)	Complaint
Plaintiffs,	)	
	)	
v.	)	
	)	
Charles T. Shrackle and	)	
The Shrackle Construction Company,	)	
	)	
Defendants.	)	

Plaintiff, Jeffrey T. Potter, individually and as administrator of the Estate of Katherine Potter, complains against Defendants, Charles T. Shrackle and Shrackle Construction Company, as follows:

FIRST CLAIM FOR RELIEF

1. Plaintiff was, and still is, a resident of Darrow County, Nita.

2. Defendant Charles T. Shrackle was, and still is, a resident of Darrow County, Nita, and the Defendant Shrackle Construction Company was, and still is, doing business in Darrow County, Nita.

3. Katherine Potter died on December 4, 2017.

4. Plaintiff and Katherine Potter were married at the time of her death and had been married for twelve years.

5. Plaintiff has been duly appointed the Administrator of Katherine Potter's estate.

6. On November 30, 2017, at about 3:30 p.m., Katherine Potter was walking in an easterly direction across Mattis Avenue at the intersection of Mattis and Kirby Avenues in Nita City, Nita.

7. At this time and place Defendant Charles T. Shrackle was driving a 2003 Toyota pickup truck, which struck Katherine Potter, causing her serious injuries and death as a result of such injuries on December 4, 2017.

8.   The truck driven by Defendant Charles T. Shrackle was owned by the Defendant Shrackle Construction Company, and at the time Katherine Potter was struck by the truck, Charles T. Shrackle was performing duties for and acting on behalf of the Shrackle Construction Company.

9.   Defendant Charles T. Shrackle was driving the Toyota pickup truck in a careless, negligent, and reckless manner, and in violation of his duties under Nita Revised Statutes 89-12(4)(2017) to exercise due care to avoid striking the pedestrian Katherine Potter who was then lawfully walking across the street.

10.   Defendant Charles T. Shrackle carelessly, negligently, and in violation of Nita Revised Statutes 89-12(4)(2017) failed to keep a proper lookout, to heed the fact that Katherine Potter was crossing the street in the immediate path of his truck, or to take any action to avoid striking Katherine Potter.

11.   Defendant Charles T. Shrackle carelessly, negligently, and in violation of Nita Revised Statutes 89-12(4)(2017) failed to give proper warning of the sudden and unexpected approach of his truck either by sounding the horn or giving any other signal or warning.

12.   Defendant Charles T. Shrackle's negligence caused Katherine Potter to suffer severe physical and mental pain and suffering from the date such injuries were incurred on November 30, 2017, until her death on December 4, 2017.

13.   Defendant Charles T. Shrackle's negligence caused Katherine Potter to incur reasonable expenses for medical, hospital, and surgical care, and the loss of wages from the time of the collision until her death, in the sum of $107,800.

14.   Defendant Charles T. Shrackle's negligence caused Jeffrey T. Potter, as personal representative of the Estate of Katherine Potter, to incur reasonable funeral and burial expenses, in the sum of $16,500.

SECOND CLAIM FOR RELIEF

15.   Plaintiff realleges paragraphs 1 through 11.

16.   Defendant Charles T. Shrackle's negligence caused Jeffrey T. Potter, as the surviving spouse of Katherine Potter, to suffer damages for the loss of:

(a)   The reasonable expected net income of Katherine Potter;

(b)   Services, protection, care, and assistance of Katherine Potter, whether voluntary or obligatory, to Jeffrey T. Potter;

(c)   Society, companionship, comfort, guidance, kindly offices, and advice of Katherine Potter to Jeffrey T. Potter.

WHEREFORE, Plaintiff demands judgment against Defendants, jointly and severally, in an amount in excess of $50,000, together with interest thereon and his costs herein, and for such other relief as the Court deems just and proper.

JURY DEMAND

Plaintiff demands a trial by jury in this action.

MADDEN & JAMES

by

William James

Attorneys for Plaintiff
Suite 720, Nita Bank Building
Nita City, Nita 99994
(555) 555-0003

DATED: April 5, 2019

IN THE CIRCUIT COURT OF
DARROW COUNTY, NITA
CIVIL DIVISION

Jeffrey T. Potter, the Administrator of the Estate of Katherine Potter, and Jeffrey T. Potter, individually, Plaintiffs, v. Charles T. Shrackle and The Shrackle Construction Company, Defendants.	)))))))))))))))	Answer

Defendants for their Answer to Plaintiff's Complaint:

1. Admit the allegations contained in paragraphs 1–5, 7–8.

2. Admit that on November 30, 2017, at or about 3:30 p.m., Katherine Potter was crossing Mattis Avenue somewhere near the intersection of Kirby and Mattis Avenues. Defendants deny all other allegations in paragraph 6.

3. Deny the allegations contained in paragraphs 9–14, 16.

FIRST AFFIRMATIVE DEFENSE

4. Any injuries sustained or suffered by Katherine Potter at the time and place mentioned in the Complaint were caused, in whole or in part, or were contributed to, by the negligence of Katherine Potter and not by any negligence of Charles T. Shrackle.

SECOND AFFIRMATIVE DEFENSE

5. Katherine Potter violated Nita Revised Statutes 89-12(4)(2017) by failing to cross the street in the marked pedestrian crosswalk, to keep a proper lookout for vehicles using the roadway, and to yield the right of way to any such vehicles.

WHEREFORE, Defendants demand that judgment be entered in favor of the Defendants with the costs and disbursements of this action.

PIERCE, JOHNSON & CLARK

by

James Barber

Attorneys for Defendants
Nita National Bank Plaza
Nita City, Nita 99994
(555) 555-6207

DATED: May 3, 2019

Confidential Materials for Defendant's Law Firm (Shrackle's Counsel)

SUMMARY OF DEPOSITION OF CHARLES T. SHRACKLE

1   I am Charles T. Shrackle, one of the defendants in this case. I live at 1701 West Johnston,
2   Nita City. I am thirty-eight years old.
3
4   I am a self-employed excavating contractor. I started my business, the Shrackle Construc-
5   tion Company, four years ago. Before that time, I worked for various construction firms as a
6   supervisor. Shrackle is a small business corporation. My wife Emily and I are the only stock-
7   holders. We dig trenches for dry wells, sewer or water pipes, or for electrical conduits, and
8   install the pipes or other hardware necessary for the jobs. Then we anchor the job, usually
9   with cement, and after the work is checked and approved, refill the excavation. The firm only
10   does excavation work. We work for developers, for public utilities, and for state and local
11   government. We have twelve full-time employees, and hire a number of laborers each day
12   depending on what work we are doing. We may have as many as fifteen extra people work-
13   ing for us on any given day. Although much of our equipment is rented to fit our needs for
14   particular jobs, we own some, including a backhoe and a couple of dump trucks. We have
15   an excavator and bulldozer on one-year leases. On November 30, 2017, we were involved
16   in a couple of sewer excavation projects. One was a relatively small one for the city at the
17   corner of John and Holiday Park at the north end of town. The other was a very large project
18   for an extension of the Greenbriar Manor subdivision. Greenbriar Manor is on the south
19   end of town. This project has been giving us some problems. We were past the due date for
20   completion of our portion of the job. It wasn't our fault. We ran into some rock we hadn't
21   expected to find but the general contractor, Clark Poe, was not particularly sympathetic. In
22   fact, Poe had summoned me to a meeting on the afternoon of the accident. He had emailed
23   me asking to meet with him, which was a little unusual. Exhibit 23 is that email. We were
24   supposed to meet at the site at about 3:30. Exhibit 24 is the reply email I sent back to him.
25
26   On the morning of the accident, I got up at 6:45 a.m., my usual time. I had gotten a good
27   night's sleep, probably about seven hours. I was taking no medication and the state of my
28   health was good. I had not had any alcoholic beverages either on the day of the accident or
29   on the day before. I don't use drugs of any kind.
30
31   I started the day at my office, which is in Sommers Township, just at the northeast part of
32   town. I called my crews on my cell phone and got them organized and working, then went
33   to the John and Holiday Park site. I stayed there most of the day. We were putting the finish-
34   ing touches on a sewer we had installed. I left at about 2:30 p.m. because I had to make a
35   stop at Nita Builders Supply, which is located near downtown—a couple of miles from the
36   Holiday Park site. I ordered some material there and got to talking with some of the staff
37   and other customers. One contractor was complaining about how bad business was and
38   how much trouble he was having with some of his subcontractors. He wanted advice on
39   how to cut their charges and how to get them to get their work done on schedule. I realized
40   I was running a little late for my meeting with Poe at Greenbriar, so I cut the conversation
41   short and headed for Greenbriar. I was by myself.

1 Greenbriar is located on South Mattis Street, about five miles from where the accident
2 occurred. I would guess I left Builders Supply about ten after three.

Page 22

11. Q. What did you do once you left Builders Supply?

12. A. I drove down First Street heading out of town. When I got to Kirby I turned right.

13. Q. How long did that take?

14. A. It's about a half mile to Kirby, so I'd say no more than five or ten minutes.

15. Q. Once you turned onto Kirby, what did you do?

16. A. I went straight to Mattis so I could turn and head out to Greenbriar. Mattis is
17.   about ten blocks down the way.

18. Q. Did you use your cell phone during this time at all?

19. A. Yes. When I turned onto Kirby, I called Poe on my cell phone to tell him
20.   I would be a little bit late.

21. Q. Tell me about that conversation.

22. A. It was a quick call, less than a minute. Poe told me not to sweat being a
23.   little late, but he did say he had to leave for an appointment at 4:00
24.   so I should get there as soon as I could.

25. Q. Were you still on the phone when you arrived at Mattis?

26. A. I'm not sure. I may have still been talking to him when I got there.

36 The intersection of Mattis and Kirby is about a mile down from where I turned onto
37 Kirby. The light was green. There was moderate traffic. I did not come to a complete stop,
38 but slowed for a car that went by before I could make a left turn to go south on Mattis.
39 I started my turn from the southernmost westbound lane of Kirby. Exhibit 16 shows the
40 left-turn lane I was in on the right side of the photograph, and the median I drove around
41 on Mattis on the left side of the photo. Exhibit 11 shows cars making the same turn
42 I made from Kirby onto Mattis.
43
44 I made a gradual turn to the east, southbound lane of Mattis. I saw some schoolchildren,
45 three I think, on the southwest corner of the intersection—where Jim Marshall's car wash
46 is. They were just standing there. I had my eye on them in case one should dart into the
47 path of the car. I didn't know any of the kids and I don't remember much else about them.

1   I think I also saw a crossing guard on the corner by White Castle. I don't remember any
2   other pedestrians.
3
4   I remember making the turn and there was the impact and that was it. The impact took
5   place several seconds after I passed south of the Kirby Avenue sidewalk. I was on the inside
6   lane probably about four feet away from the median.
7
8   I did not see Ms. Potter before the impact. I did not apply my brakes before the impact,
9   although as I made the turn I had my foot on the brake pedal. I usually make my left turns
10 that way. I was probably traveling about fifteen miles an hour at the time of the impact.
11
12 I remember that it was a clear day and that the sun was out. I had to squint as I was making
13 the turn because Mattis at that point goes southwest and at that time of day the sun was
14 pretty low in the sky. I could still see in front of me. I had my eye on the children on the corner
15 all the time.
16
17 I both heard and felt the impact, but I didn't immediately know what I had hit. The impact
18 was on the left front of my vehicle. As soon as I felt the impact, I applied the brakes with
19 as much force as I could. As I said, my foot was already on the brake. The vehicle stopped
20 quickly and I jumped out. I moved around the front of the car and I saw Ms. Potter lying
21 under it. She was lying almost straight, with her head under the front bumper and her
22 feet straight back. Her head was pointed south and her feet north. She seemed to be con-
23 scious, and I asked her, "Where did you come from?" She didn't reply.
24
25 The police arrived almost immediately. We got a first-aid kit out of my truck and applied
26 a compress to her forehead and we waited for the ambulance to come. There were skid
27 marks and the police measured them. There was a mark on the left-hand side of the hood
28 of my truck, near the division between the hood and the fender.
29
30 At the time of the accident I was driving my 2003 Toyota Tacoma truck. My truck was in good
31 condition at the time of the accident. It had been inspected and the brakes checked about
32 a month before the accident. The tires were relatively new. I think they had less than
33 5,000 miles on them. Exhibit 6 shows me and my truck at a job site out in Ferndale just
34 after I got it. Yeah, I am talking on my cell phone in that picture—it seems like half this
35 job is solving problems and coordinating jobs on the phone. The logo shown on the truck
36 in that exhibit, and more closely in Exhibit 7, is my company logo.
37
38 At the time of the accident, I was covered by an automobile liability policy of $500,000
39 per person and $1 million per accident. The policy was with Boston Casualty. The policy
40 number is FA606560, effective September 23, 2017, to September 23, 2019. Except for
41 the fact that there is concern that this action will exceed the policy limits, the insur-
42 ance company hasn't indicated any problem with my coverage. I also have a $5 million
43 umbrella policy for the company with Boston Casualty. They have also been notified
44 about this accident.

1   I did not meet with Clark Poe at Greenbriar that day. Shortly after they took Ms. Potter
2   away in the ambulance, I texted him saying what happened and why I didn't get there as
3   promised. (Exhibit 33 is that text.) We met the next day. Based on our conversation, there
4   was a reduction in the amount we were to be paid for the job. I wasn't too happy about
5   the result, but compared to Ms. Potter's situation it was no big deal.

6

7   Ordinarily it would take me about twenty minutes to get from Builders Supply to Greenbrier.
8   However, it could take longer on weekday afternoons about that time because of the
9   schools getting out. The traffic was a little heavy before I got to the intersection of Kirby
10   and Mattis, but not too bad. I thought that it might get worse after I turned on Mattis,
11   particularly down about a mile when the road narrows. It's highway at that point, but two
12   lanes. But I felt I'd make it in plenty of time for my meeting with Poe.

13

14   I have read the foregoing and it is a true and accurate transcription of my deposition testi-
15   mony given on May 16, 2019.

Signed: _Charles T. Shrackle_   Date: <u>May 16, 2019</u>

         Charles T. Shrackle

Subscribed and sworn before me this 16th day of May, 2019.

Terry Anderson

Terry Anderson
Notary

SUMMARY OF DEPOSITION OF ALICE MALLORY

1   My name is Alice Mallory. I am forty-seven years old. I am married and have two children,
2   both of whom are in high school. I work part-time as a school crossing guard at the corner
3   of Mattis and Kirby. I have done that work for about two years. I work both in the morn-
4   ing and in the afternoon at that corner.
5
6   On the afternoon of November 30, 2017, I was working on the southwest corner of the
7   intersection. At about 3:25, I crossed over to the southeast corner of the street by the
8   White Castle to reprimand a small boy who had not heeded my warning to stop. He had
9   run out in front of some cars but luckily wasn't hurt. I was extremely upset by the inci-
10   dent. The boy could have been killed. It would be the worst thing I could imagine—a child
11   being killed while I was the guard. Exhibit 9 shows where I started out in the foreground,
12   and also where I was in front of the White Castle when I saw Ms. Potter across the street.
13   As I knelt to talk to him, I saw a woman in my peripheral vision—I later learned this was
14   Ms. Katherine Potter. She crossed the street from west to east in the crosswalk. I can't
15   remember what she was wearing or much about her, but I remember that she had dark hair.
16
17   When she reached the median, she suddenly turned south and began to walk south on the
18   median strip. I looked down to continue talking to the boy. then heard a thump and looked
19   up instantly. I saw Ms. Potter being carried on the hood of a pickup truck about thirty feet
20   south of the crosswalk. The truck stopped about twenty feet later. I ran over to see if I could
21   help, but others got there before me, so I returned to looking after the children.
22
23   At the time I was watching Ms. Potter, I was also watching children on the other corner.
24   I was really concerned that one of them would cross the street in a dangerous way.
25   However, I did see clearly all that I have said here. I did not come forward as a witness
26   originally because I was upset and didn't want my story to hurt Ms. Potter or her family.
27   I was finally contacted by the defendant's lawyer and told her what I saw.
28
29   Three weeks after this incident, just before Christmas, I resigned my position as a school
30   crossing guard. The tension of looking after children was too much for me. I guess I was
31   also affected by Ms. Potter's accident and death.
32
33   Also, my eyesight has become worse. I have a degenerative eye condition that will get
34   progressively worse as I age. I still see pretty well with corrective lenses and feel that
35   I could have kept on as a guard for a little longer. However, the pressure of concern for
36   the children and the trauma of the accident caused me to quit early.
37
38   Yes, I was wearing my corrective lenses at the time of the accident. My sight is normal
39   with those lenses although there are some limits to my peripheral vision. I have what is
40   known as primary open-angle glaucoma. It was undiagnosed for a long time and hadn't
41   been diagnosed at the time of the accident. They discovered that my central vision is

1 fine, but that I have some weakening peripheral vision. It was just starting to be a prob-
2 lem at the time of the accident. I had surgery about two months ago that my doctor says
3 will correct most of the problem.

I have read the foregoing and it is a true and accurate transcription of my deposition testimony given on June 13, 2019.

Signed: *Alice Mallory* .   Date: <u>June 13, 2019</u>

Alice Mallory

Signed and sworn to before me this 13th day of June, 2019.

Able Ames

Able Ames
Notary

SUMMARY OF DEPOSITION OF JUANITA WILLIAMS

1   My name is Juanita Williams. I live at 1010 West Kirby, Unit 15, in Nita City. I work part-
2   time as a secretary. I am a single mother with two children, Victoria, age ten and Joshua,
3   age three.
4
5   On November 30, 2017, at approximately 3:30 p.m., I was at the corner of Kirby and Mattis.
6   I was stopped on Kirby Avenue, west of the intersection, facing east getting ready for the
7   light to change to green. I had just picked up Victoria at Senn School and was driving my
8   green 2015 Toyota Highlander to pick up Josh at his day care.
9
10 A man in a pickup truck was in the left-hand lane of westbound Kirby on the opposite side
11 of the intersection with his left turn signal on as he was waiting to turn southwest on Mattis.
12 It looked like he was talking on his cell phone or he may have simply had his hand up to his
13 ear. The light changed to green, he waited until I had passed, and with the light still green
14 he turned southwest on Mattis. The pickup truck took the turn a little fast, maybe at about
15 twenty miles an hour. He sort of rolled through the intersection and then picked up speed.
16
17 I actually didn't see him hit the dark-haired woman, who I later found out was Ms. Potter,
18 but he could not have been going fast because I was only a few feet from the intersection
19 when my daughter screamed, "Mom, someone was just hit." We immediately turned
20 around and went back to the accident.
21
22 When we went back to the intersection and parked at the White Castle, I saw the dark-haired
23 woman lying underneath the pickup truck. I saw that funny Superman logo on the truck.
24
25 I didn't know Ms. Potter or anyone in her family. I don't know Charles Shrackle and
26 I never heard of Shrackle Construction Company until the time of the accident.

I have read the foregoing and it is a true and accurate transcription of my deposition testimony given on June 12, 2019.

Signed: _Juanita Williams_   Date: _June 12, 2019_

Juanita Williams

Signed and sworn to before me this 12th day of June, 2019.

Joseph Lucey

Joseph Lucey
Notary

SUMMARY OF DEPOSITION OF VICTORIA WILLIAMS

1   My name is Vicky Williams, and I am ten years old. I live at 1010 W. Kirby Avenue in Nita
2   City with my mom and my brother, Joshua. Joshua is three.
3
4   My mom was driving me home from school on November 30, 2017. She always picks me up.
5   I was in the back seat in the car on the passenger side. I don't remember if I had my seat belt
6   on but I usually do. I think it was about 3:30 in the afternoon when the accident happened.
7
8   We were headed toward town on Kirby Avenue. On the map you showed me that would be
9   going east. (Exhibit 3) We stopped for a light where Kirby crosses Mattis near the White
10 Castle. There was a man in a truck coming towards us on the opposite side of the inter-
11 section getting ready to make a left turn onto Mattis. I was looking out the side window at
12 some of my school friends who were on the sidewalk in front of the car wash. There were
13 three or four of them. I waved and smiled at my friends trying to get their attention.
14
15 Mom started driving across the intersection. I twisted around to look out the back window
16 and saw the man in the truck turn after we passed him. I saw him because I was looking
17 towards my friends. A lady with black or brown hair, I think, was standing on the center strip
18 on Mattis a little down from the crosswalk. She was facing towards my friends with her back
19 to us. She just stepped right off the center strip right in front of the truck. I saw the truck
20 hit her and her purse went flying into the air. The truck screeched his brakes and stopped.
21 You're right that the sun was a little in my eyes but I could see what happened to the lady.
22 I probably just put my hand up to my forehead so I could see my friends even though the
23 sun was out, but I really don't remember. I know I could see what I told you about.
24
25 I yelled to my mom about what just happened, that the truck hit someone. She turned
26 around and we went back and parked in the White Castle parking lot. I saw the lady that
27 got hit lying underneath the truck. It was pretty scary.

Page 14

11. Q. Where was the woman when you first saw her?

12. A. She was down the crosswalk on Mattis.

13. Q. Do you mean south of the crosswalk?

14. A. I'm not too good with directions. She was away from Kirby Street.

15. Q. How many feet was she away from Kirby?

16. A. I'm not too good with guessing feet. I would say maybe twenty feet.

17. Q. Could it have been less?

18. A. Maybe, but I'd say about twenty. Fifteen or twenty.

19. Q. How wide is Mattis Avenue at that point?

20. A. Gee, I don't know. Probably a couple of hundred feet wide.

9 I looked at the map and picture that you called Exhibit 17, and it shows about where we
10 were and what I could see when I first saw the lady standing on the center strip. The map
11 and picture that you called Exhibit 18 shows about where we were when I saw the purse
12 flying in the air.

I have read the foregoing and it is a true and accurate transcription of my deposition testimony given on May 12, 2019.

Signed: *Victoria Williams*   Date: <u>May 12, 2019</u>
Victoria Williams

Signed and sworn to before me this 12th day of May, 2019.

Joseph Lucey

Joseph Lucey
Notary

SUMMARY OF DEPOSITION OF BENJAMIN GRIMSON

1 My name is Benjamin Grimson. I just turned nineteen years old. I am presently in prison at
2 Allenwood Prison in Allenwood, Nita.
3
4 On November 30 last year, I was cruising down Mattis in a Camry when I stopped for a
5 burger and fries at the White Castle on Kirby. My buddy, Eddie, works there and he waited
6 on me at the drive-through after I placed my order. As I was heading away from the drive-
7 through window, I heard a loud thump and when I looked over there was this lady flying in
8 the air on the front of a truck. I yelled, "Holy shit, somebody smashed up that lady." When
9 I saw her she was in mid-air. At that point, I'd say she was about ten feet south of the cross-
10 walk. The truck must have carried her another thirty-five feet or so. When I saw the truck
11 carrying her, it looked like it was still going pretty fast, maybe twenty miles an hour. The truck
12 stopped and the driver got out of the truck. He said something but I couldn't hear what it
13 was. A bunch of people ran over to her. I decided there wasn't anything I could do. There
14 wasn't anybody behind me, so I backed up and went out the Kirby Street entrance.
15
16 I drove a couple of blocks east on Kirby and pulled into a parking space on the street. I ate
17 my hamburger and texted Eddie. (Exhibit 32 is that text.)
18
19 The picture that says Exhibit 19 shows the drive-through lane at the White Castle. Exhibit 20
20 shows what you can see of Mattis Avenue from further down the drive-through lane. That's
21 where I was when I saw this lady.
22
23 Eddie must have told somebody I had been at the drive-through window when the acci-
24 dent occurred. He also told you where to find me.
25
26 On February 25, 2019, I was arrested for grand larceny automobile. I was charged as an
27 adult with the theft of several cars, including the 2015 Toyota Camry I was driving when
28 I saw the accident. The car belonged to one of the teachers at my high school. I am now
29 serving a sentence of two years at Allenwood, which is a minimum security Nita prison.

I have read the foregoing and it is a true and accurate transcription of my deposition testimony given on June 17, 2019.

Signed: ___Benjamin Grimson___   Date: June 17, 2019

Benjamin Grimson

Subscribed and sworn to before me this 17th day of June, 2019.

___Tracy Williams___

Tracy Williams
Notary

Materials Available to Both Sides

Expert Report of Robert Glenn, PhD
Professor of Economics
University of Nita

State of Nita Circuit Court
Circuit Court of Darrow County
Civil Division

Jeffrey T. Potter, the Administrator of the Estate of Katherine Potter,
and Jeffrey T. Potter, individually
(Plaintiff)

v.

Charles T. Shrackle and The Shrackle Construction Company
(Defendants)

Dated: July 1, 2019

Introduction

I, Robert Glenn, understand this matter involves Jeffrey T. Potter, the Administrator of the Estate of Katherine Potter, and Jeffrey T. Potter, individually, as plaintiff, and Charles T. Shrackle and The Shrackle Construction Company (collectively, "Shrackle") as defendants. As I understand this matter, Ms. Katherine Potter was struck by an automobile driven by Mr. Charles T. Shrackle on November 30, 2017. Ms. Potter died on December 4, 2017, as a result of injuries sustained in that accident.

Engagement of Robert Glenn

As part of this engagement, Madden & James, counsel for plaintiffs, requested that I:
1. Review the Potter v. Shrackle case file, including but not limited to:
   a. the complaint and answer;
   b. statements of Marilyn J. Kelly, Juanita Williams, Victoria Williams, Alice Mallory, and Benjamin Grimson;
   c. depositions of James Marshall, Victoria Williams, Michael Young, Charles T. Shrackle, Jeffrey Potter, and Daniel Sloan; and
   d. other documents provided by counsel;
2. Collect information relevant to a calculation of economic losses resulting from a wrongful death; and
3. Provide economic and statistical analysis regarding plaintiff's specific claims.

In preparing my analysis, I have relied on counsel, Madden & James, for any interpretation of legal issues.

Supplemental Analysis and Opinions

I understand that discovery in this matter is still ongoing and that additional documents, statements, depositions, or trial testimony on topics relevant to the opinions issued in this report may be forthcoming. As a result, I reserve the right to supplement this report or to address any such testimony at trial.

Opinion

Based upon my continuing review and analysis of the Potter v. Shrackle case file, supplemented with my own research of relevant economic and demographic information, I have developed the following opinion regarding economic damages in this matter.
1. From the date of her death through her eventual retirement at age 60, the value of Katherine Potter's lost earnings, benefits and household work, and net of her consumption is a loss of $2,334,579 to her estate and to her husband, Jeffrey Potter. In present discounted value, this amount is a loss of $1,532,021 to the plaintiff.

Bases for Opinions

1. Katherine Potter was in good health at the time of her death and would have reasonably been expected to work until at least the age of 60 before her retirement.
2. Katherine Potter was happy with her position as a Technology Training Specialist at Techno-Soft, Inc. I believe the pattern of her salary growth from the date of her death to

her eventual retirement at age 60 would be similar to the average pattern of salary growth during her period of employment with the company.

3. Katherine Potter would have continued to enjoy her fringe benefits as an employee of Techno-Soft, Inc. I have spoken with Ms. Linda Graham, Human Resources Director at Techno-Soft, Inc. and have learned that Katherine Potter's benefits amounted to 20 percent of her income at the time of her death.
4. Katherine Potter shared equally in the household work with her husband, Jeffrey Potter, and her death will result in a loss equal to the value of Katherine's labor, which equaled approximately $41 per hour at the date of her death.

Exhibits

For purposes of presenting our opinions and their bases, I may develop and use exhibits including overheads, flip charts, and other summary graphics. I may also use certain demonstrative aids and illustrations in presenting technical concepts and analyses.

Compensation

The hourly rates for myself and my research associates who worked on this matter range between $75 and $350 per hour. My hourly rate is $350 per hour.

Qualifications

I am a Professor of Economics at the University of Nita in Nita City with fields of concentration in labor economics and microeconomics. I hold a bachelors degree in economics from the University of North Carolina (2000) and a PhD in economics from the University of Illinois (2004). I have taught economics at the undergraduate and graduate level at the University of Nita for fourteen years as well as numerous seminars in the industry. As part of my duties as a professor at a research institution, I direct graduate research, conduct independent research, and publish my results in academic economic journals. In addition to my publications, I have received research grants from the National Science Foundation, the Social Science Research Council, the Center for Comparative Studies at the University of Nita, and the Nita Law Enforcement Commission.

July 1, 2019

Robert Glenn
Professor of Economics, University of Nita

POTTER V. SHRACKLE AND THE SHRACKLE CONSTRUCTION COMPANY
DAMAGES MODEL OF ROBERT GLENN, PhD

TABLE 1. SUMMARY OF ECONOMIC LOSS, WRONGFUL DEATH OF KATHERINE POTTER

Summary of Economic Loss

		Nominal Dollars	Present Discounted Value
A.	Future Value of Earnings	$2,918,363	$1,915,118
B.	Future Value of Fringe Benefits	$583,673	$383,024
C.	Future Value of Household Work	$1,024,233	$672,133
D.	Future Value of Personal Consumption	$2,191,691	$1,438,254
E.	Total Value of Loss (A + B + C - D)	$2,334,579	$1,532,021

POTTER V. SHRACKLE AND THE SHRACKLE CONSTRUCTION COMPANY
DAMAGES MODEL OF ROBERT GLENN, PhD

TABLE 2. FUTURE VALUE OF EARNINGS OF KATHERINE POTTER AGE 45 TO 60

Date of Birth: June 15, 1972
Date of Death: December 4, 2017
Appraisal Period: 2019 – 2031
Projected Retirement Age: 60
Discount Rate: 6.00%
Earnings Growth Rate: 9.80%

Year	Projected Age	Projected Value Earnings	Present Discounted Value of Earnings
2017	45	$85,000	
2018	46	$93,329	$93,329
2019	47	$102,474	$102,474
2020	48	$112,515	$106,146
2021	49	$123,540	$109,950
2022	50	$135,645	$113,890
2023	51	$148,936	$117,971
2024	52	$163,530	$122,199
2025	53	$179,554	$126,578
2026	54	$197,147	$131,114
2027	55	$216,465	$135,813
2028	56	$237,676	$140,680
2029	57	$260,965	$145,721
2030	58	$286,536	$150,943
2031	59	$314,612	$156,353
2032	60	$345,440	$161,956
Value of Future Earnings:		$2,918,363	$1,915,118

POTTER V. SHRACKLE AND THE SHRACKLE CONSTRUCTION COMPANY
DAMAGES MODEL OF ROBERT GLENN, PhD

TABLE 3. HISTORICAL EARNINGS GROWTH OF KATHERINE POTTER, 1993 TO 2017

Date of Birth: June 15, 1972
Date of Death: December 4, 2017
Observation Period: 1993 to 2017

Year	Age	Earnings	% Change from Previous Year	Job
1994 to 1996	22-24	$0	n/a	(1)
1997	25	$19,000	n/a	(2)
1998	26	$19,600	3.2%	(2)
1999	27	$20,250	3.3%	(2)
2000	28	$20,900	3.2%	(2)
2001	29	$21,600	3.3%	(2)
2002	30	$22,300	3.2%	(2)
2003	31	$23,000	3.1%	(2)
2004	32	$23,750	3.3%	(2)
2005	33	$24,500	3.2%	(2)
2006	34	$25,400	3.7%	(2)/(3)
2007	35	$34,000	33.9%	(3)
2008	36	$42,000	23.5%	(3)
2009	37	$50,000	19.0%	(3)
2010	38	$57,500	15.0%	(3)
2011	39	$62,500	8.7%	(3)
2012	40	$67,500	8.0%	(3)
2013	41	$71,000	5.2%	(3)
2014	42	$73,500	3.5%	(3)
2015	43	$76,000	3.4%	(3)
2016	44	$78,000	2.6%	(3)
2017	45	$85,000	9.0%	(3)
2018	Deceased	$0	100.0%	Deceased

Average Income Growth Rate (2006 to 2016): 9.80%

Job Information:

(1) Attending Graduate School, University of Nita
(2) Computer Instructor, Nita City Unified School District
(3) Computer Instructor, Techno-Soft, Inc.

POTTER V. SHRACKLE AND THE SHRACKLE CONSTRUCTION COMPANY
DAMAGES MODEL OF ROBERT GLENN, PhD

TABLE 4. FUTURE VALUE OF FRINGE BENEFITS OF KATHERINE POTTER, AGE 45 TO 60

Date of Birth:	June 15, 1972
Date of Death:	December 4, 2017
Appraisal Period:	2017 to 2031
Projected Retirement Age:	60
Discount Rate:	6.00%
Benefits as % of Income:	20.00%

Year	Projected Age	Projected Value of Fringe Benefits	Present Discounted Value of Fringe Benefits
2016	45	$17,000	
2017	46	$18,666	$18,666
2018	47	$20,495	$20,495
2019	48	$22,503	$21,229
2020	49	$24,708	$21,990
2021	50	$27,129	$22,778
2022	51	$29,787	$23,594
2023	52	$32,706	$24,440
2024	53	$35,911	$25,316
2025	54	$39,429	$26,223
2026	55	$43,293	$27,163
2027	56	$47,535	$28,136
2028	57	$52,193	$29,144
2029	58	$57,307	$30,189
2030	59	$62,922	$31,271
2031	60	$69,088	$32,391
Value of Future Fringe Benefits:		$583,673	$383,024

POTTER V. SHRACKLE AND THE SHRACKLE CONSTRUCTION COMPANY
DAMAGES MODEL OF ROBERT GLENN, PhD

TABLE 5. FUTURE VALUE OF HOUSEHOLD WORK OF KATHERINE POTTER, AGE 45 TO 60

Date of Birth:	June 15, 1972
Date of Death:	December 4, 2017
Appraisal Period:	2019 to 2031
Projected Retirement Age:	60
Discount Rate:	6.00%
# of Hours Per Day at Household Work:	2
Days Per Year Doing Household Work:	365

Year	Projected Age	Projected Value of Household Work	Present Discounted Value of Household Work
2017	45	$29,832	
2018	46	$32,755	$32,755
2019	47	$35,964	$35,964
2020	48	$39,488	$37,253
2021	49	$43,358	$38,588
2022	50	$47,606	$39,971
2023	51	$52,271	$41,403
2024	52	$57,393	$42,887
2025	53	$63,016	$44,424
2026	54	$69,191	$46,016
2027	55	$75,971	$47,665
2028	56	$83,415	$49,373
2028	57	$91,589	$51,143
2030	58	$100,563	$52,975
2031	59	$110,417	$54,874
2032	60	$121,236	$56,840
Value of Future Household Work:		$1,024,233	$672,133

Assumption:

(1) There are 2,080 work hours in a year (52 weeks * 40 hours per week).

**POTTER V. SHRACKLE AND THE SHRACKLE CONSTRUCTION COMPANY
DAMAGES MODEL OF ROBERT GLENN, PhD**

**TABLE 6. FUTURE VALUE OF PERSONAL CONSUMPTION
OF KATHERINE POTTER, AGE 45 TO 60**

Date of Birth:	June 15, 1972
Date of Death:	December 4, 2017
Appraisal Period:	2019 to 2031
Projected Retirement Age:	60
Discount Rate:	6.00%
Consumption as % of Income:	75.10%

Year	Projected Age	*Projected Value of Personal Consumption*	*Present Discounted Value of Personal Consumption*
2017	45	$63,835	
2018	46	$70,090	$70,090
2019	47	$76,958	$76,958
2020	48	$84,499	$79,716
2021	49	$92,778	$82,572
2022	50	$101,869	$85,531
2023	51	$111,851	$88,597
2024	52	$122,811	$91,772
2025	53	$134,845	$95,060
2026	54	$148,058	$98,467
2027	55	$162,565	$101,996
2028	56	$178,495	$105,651
2029	57	$195,985	$109,437
2030	58	$215,188	$113,359
2031	59	$236,274	$117,421
2032	60	$259,425	$121,629
Value of Future Consumption:		$2,191,691	$1,438,254

**POTTER V. SHRACKLE AND THE SHRACKLE CONSTRUCTION COMPANY
DAMAGES MODEL OF ROBERT GLENN, PhD**

**TABLE 6. FUTURE VALUE OF PERSONAL CONSUMPTION
OF KATHERINE POTTER, AGE 45 TO 60**

TABLE 6 NOTES

(1) To arrive at Katherine Potter's net contribution to the Potter household welfare (i.e., what Jeffrey Potter will lose monetarily as a result of his wife's death), the future value of Katherine's consumption expenditures should be subtracted from the future value of her income, fringe benefits, and household work.

(2) The U.S. Department of Labor has calculated that, on average, household expenditures amount to 89.1 percent of household income for American households.

(3) Of this amount, on average, 28 percent of household income is spent on housing expenses.

(4) In this matter, half of this amount should be excluded from Katherine Potter's share of income spent on household expenses since housing is a benefit equally shared by both Katherine and Jeffrey Potter. Katherine's death is a loss to Mr. Potter insofar as Katherine contributed to the cost of housing for their household.

(5) As a result, 75.1 percent of Katherine's future wage and salary earnings should be subtracted from her total wage and salary earnings to account for the value of her expenditures.

Source: State of NITA Department of Labor, Consumer Expenditures in 2017, May 2019.

Robert Glenn, PhD
Goldman Sachs Professor of Economics
University of Nita, Department of Economics, Campus Locator #43
Nita City, Nita
(555) 444-2308, Fax (555) 444-2307
glennecon@email.nita.edu

Education

BS University of North Carolina (1998) (economics)
PhD University of Illinois (2003) (economics)

Employment History

Assistant Professor, University of Nita, 2003–2009
Associate Professor, University of Nita, 2009–2013
Professor, University of Nita, 2013–2019
Goldman Sachs Professor, 2019–

Principal Publications since 2007:

Books

Microeconomics in a Time of Terrorism, Oxford University Press (2019)

Loss Evaluation in Wrongful Death Cases, Aspen (2015)

Articles

"The Effect of September 11 on Microeconomic Theory," 80 *Harvard Public Policy Review* 1769 (2019)

"Is Your Loss Worth Anything?" 5 *Journal of Law and Economics* 1289 (2015)

"Can Our Economic System Survive a Terrorist Attack?" 45 *Economics and Politics* 549 (2014)

"Valuing Services and Potential Retirement," 19 *Journal of Labor Economics* 42 (2010)

Sample Expert Testimony

(I have been qualified as an expert in economics in 24 different cases. I have testified for the plaintiff in all but three cases.)

Michaels v. Hammer, North Carolina Superior Court, October 2019 (personal injury, testified for plaintiff)

Smith v. Tucker, United States District Court (SDNY) (personal injury, testified for plaintiff)

Rosen v. Nichol, United States District Court (S. D. Calif.) (wrongful death, testified for plaintiff)

Glandon v. Schwartz, Nita Superior Court, May 2014 (wrongful death case, testified for plaintiff)

State of Nita Circuit Court Circuit Court of Darrow
County Civil Division

Jeffrey T. Potter, the Administrator of the Estate
of Katherine Potter, and Jeffrey T. Potter,
individually
(Plaintiff)

v.

Charles T. Shrackle and
The Shrackle Construction Company
(Defendants)

Expert Report of Elizabeth Buchanan, Ph.D.
Assistant Professor of Economics, Nita State University
Nita City, Nita

September 2, 2019

1.0 Introduction

I, Elizabeth Buchanan, understand this matter involves Jeffrey T. Potter, the Administrator of the Estate of Katherine Potter, and Jeffrey T. Potter, individually, as plaintiff, and Charles T. Shrackle and The Shrackle Construction Company (collectively, "Shrackle") as defendants. As I understand this matter, Ms. Katherine Potter was struck by an automobile driven by Mr. Charles T. Shrackle on November 30, 2017. Ms. Potter died on December 4, 2017, as a result of injuries sustained in that accident.

2.0 Qualifications

I am an Assistant Professor of Economics at Nita State University with fields of concentration in labor economics and industrial organization. I am also a graduate of the University of Nita, holding both a bachelors and doctorate degree in economics. I have taught at Nita State University for the past five years: two years as a visiting professor, two years as a lecturer, and one year as an assistant professor. Appendix A is a copy of my current resume. It contains a listing of my papers and publications for the past ten years.

2.1 Engagement of Elizabeth Buchanan

As part of this engagement, James Barber of Pierce, Johnson & Clark ("Pierce"), counsel for defendants Shrackle, requested that I:

- Review the expert report on damages prepared by Dr. Robert Glenn;

- Review the Potter v. Shrackle case file, including but not limited to:
  - the complaint and answer;
  - depositions of James Marshall, Victoria Williams, Michael Young, Charles T. Shrackle, Jeffrey T. Potter, and Daniel Sloan;
  - statements of Marilyn J. Kelly, Juanita Williams, Victoria Williams, Alice Mallory, Benjamin Grimson; and
  - other documents which I have reviewed which have been produced in this matter;

- Collect information relevant to a calculation of economic losses resulting from a wrongful death; and

- Provide economic and statistical analysis regarding plaintiff's specific claims.

In preparing my analysis, I have relied on counsel, Pierce, for any interpretation of legal issues.

2.2 Supplemental Analysis and Opinions

I understand that discovery in this matter is still ongoing and that additional documents, statements, deposition, or trial testimony on topics relevant to the opinions issued in this report may be forthcoming. As a result, I reserve the right to supplement this report or to address any such testimony at trial.

3.0 Opinion

Based upon my continuing review and analysis of Dr. Glenn's expert report and the Potter v. Shrackle case file, supplemented with my own research of relevant economic and demographic information, I have developed the following opinion regarding economic damages in this matter.

- Dr. Robert Glenn substantially overstates the total value of loss allegedly suffered by the plaintiff due to incorrect and inappropriate assumptions used in his damages model.

- In my own opinion, from the date of her death through her eventual retirement at age fifty-five, the value of Katherine Potter's lost earnings, benefits and household work, net of her consumption is a loss of $411,077 to her estate and to her husband, Jeffrey Potter. In present discounted value, this amount is a loss of $333,719 to the plaintiff.

4.0 Bases for Opinions

- It is my opinion that Katherine Potter would have reasonably been expected to work full-time until the age of fifty and then would work part-time until her retirement at age fifty-five. Deposition testimony from her husband, Jeffrey Potter, stated that he and Ms. Potter talked about taking an early retirement. My calculations of loss valuation is conservative in that it treats Ms. Potter as having worked to the age of fifty-five, which would tend to overstate the loss if she were to retire before that age.

- It is my opinion that Katherine Potter would have an average annual salary increase of 5 percent per year. Dr. Glenn averages Ms. Potter's salary increases during her entire period of employment at Techno-Soft, Inc. This method would overstate the salary increases Ms. Potter would likely receive in the period after her death. I note that her salary increases are smaller and smaller, in percentage terms, and thus the use of long-run averages would be ignorant of this trend. Instead, I use an average of her annual salary increases over the last three years to capture the fact that she may be reaching the upper salary limit of her position.

- I assume that the imputed value of benefits enjoyed by Katherine Potter is 17.5 percent of her annual salary. Like Dr. Glenn, I have spoken to Linda Graham, Human Resources Director at Techno-Soft, Inc. Based upon my discussion with Ms. Graham, I learned that

Dr. Glenn's calculation of future fringe benefits overstates this value since it ignores the fact that Katherine Potter received a special one-time bonus payout of $10,000 in 2017 for staying beyond ten years at Techno-Soft, Inc. Were this one-time payout to be removed, the actual rate of benefits would be lowered from 20 percent to 17.5 percent of her annual salary. Dr. Glenn thus overstates all future projections for fringe benefit calculations since he does not appropriately evaluate the baseline year. I use the more justifiable number of 17.5 percent in my projections.

- Although Katherine Potter shared equally in the household work with her husband, Jeffrey Potter, and her death will result in a loss equal to the value of Ms. Potter's labor, I disagree with Dr. Glenn's methodology of using her imputed hourly wage as the appropriate replacement wage. Ms. Potter's hourly wage, assuming a 2,080-hour work year, is imputed to be approximately $41 per hour. Dr. Glenn uses this amount as the value of Ms. Potter's lost labor. This methodology is incorrect in that Dr. Glenn should value the loss of Ms. Potter's household labor at its replacement cost. Since many of the household tasks did not require the use of Ms. Potter's specialized skills, I use a more appropriate measure of replacement cost, the minimum wage.

- It is my opinion that, as a member of the Potter household, Katherine Potter consumed approximately 75 percent of her annual income as her personal consumption. The amount of consumption that Ms. Potter consumed for her benefit out of her income should not be included in an award of damages to Mr. Potter as he did not necessarily benefit from this consumption during Ms. Potter's lifetime. Although Ms. Potter would continue to consume as a member of the household after her retirement, in order to be conservative in the estimate of damages, I exclude this amount from the calculation of loss to Mr. Potter. Inclusion of this stream of consumption of retirement would make the damages amount even smaller as Ms. Potter would continue to consume but not be earning any wage or salary income.

In sum, these inappropriate and inaccurate assumptions used by Dr. Glenn in his model result in a significant overstatement of any likely damages suffered. I believe that he may have overstated damages by as much as a factor of four. I believe that damages suffered by the plaintiff would not have exceeded $334,000.

5.0 Exhibits

For purposes of presenting our opinions and their bases, I may develop and use exhibits including overheads, flip charts, and other summary graphics. I may also use certain demonstrative aids and illustrations in presenting technical concepts and analyses.

6.0 Compensation

The hourly rates for myself and my research associates who worked on this matter range between \$50 and \$250 per hour. My hourly rate is \$250 per hour.

Elizabeth C. Buchanan

Elizabeth C. Buchanan
Assistant Professor of Economics
Nita State University
Nita City, Nita
September 2, 2019

POTTER V. SHRACKLE AND THE SHRACKLE CONSTRUCTION COMPANY REBUTTAL DAMAGES MODEL OF ELIZABETH C. BUCHANAN, PhD

TABLE 1. SUMMARY OF ECONOMIC LOSS, WRONGFUL DEATH OF KATHERINE POTTER

Summary of Economic Loss

		Nominal Dollars	*Present Discounted Value*
A.	Future Value of Earnings	$807,964	$680,250
B.	Future Value of Fringe Benefits	$141,394	$119,044
C.	Future Value of Household Work	$68,500	$45,293
D.	Future Value of Personal Consumption	$606,781	$510,868
E.	Total Value of Loss (A + B + C - D)	$411,077	$333,719

POTTER V. SHRACKLE AND THE SHRACKLE CONSTRUCTION COMPANY REBUTTAL DAMAGES MODEL OF ELIZABETH C. BUCHANAN, PhD

TABLE 2. FUTURE VALUE OF EARNINGS OF KATHERINE POTTER, AGE 45 TO 60

Date of Birth:	June 15, 1972
Date of Death:	December 4, 2017
Appraisal Period:	2019 to 2031
Projected Retirement Age:	55
Discount Rate:	6.00%
Earnings Growth Rate:	5.00%

Year	Projected Age	% of Full-Time	Projected Value of Earnings	Present Discounted Value of Earnings
2017	45	100%	$85,000	
2018	46	100%	$89,252	$89,252
2019	47	100%	$93,717	$93,717
2020	48	100%	$98,405	$92,835
2021	49	100%	$103,328	$91,961
202	50	100%	$108,497	$91,096
2023	51	50%	$56,962	$45,119
2024	52	50%	$59,811	$44,695
2025	53	50%	$62,803	$44,274
2026	54	50%	$65,945	$43,857
2027	55	50%	$69,244	$43,445
2028	56	0%	(RETIRED)	(RETIRED)
2029	57	0%	(RETIRED)	(RETIRED)
2030	58	0%	(RETIRED)	(RETIRED)
2031	59	0%	(RETIRED)	(RETIRED)
2032	60	0%	(RETIRED)	(RETIRED)
Value of Future Earnings:			$807,964	$680,250

**POTTER V. SHRACKLE AND THE SHRACKLE CONSTRUCTION COMPANY REBUTTAL
DAMAGES MODEL OF ELIZABETH C. BUCHANAN, PhD**

TABLE 3. HISTORICAL EARNINGS GROWTH OF KATHERINE POTTER, 1993 TO 2017

Date of Birth: June 15, 1972
Date of Death: December 4, 2017
Observation Period: 1993 to 2017

Year	Age	Earnings	% Change from Previous Year	Job
1994 to 1996	22-24	$0	n/a	(1)
1997	25	$19,000	n/a	(2)
1998	26	$19,600	3.2%	(2)
1999	27	$20,250	3.3%	(2)
2000	28	$20,900	3.2%	(2)
2001	29	$21,600	3.3%	(2)
2002	30	$22,300	3.2%	(2)
2003	31	$23,000	3.1%	(2)
2004	32	$23,750	3.3%	(2)
2005	33	$24,500	3.2%	(2)
2006	34	$25,400	3.7%	(2)/(3)
2007	35	$34,000	33.9%	(3)
2008	36	$42,000	23.5%	(3)
2009	37	$50,000	19.0%	(3)
2010	38	$57,500	15.0%	(3)
2011	39	$62,500	8.7%	(3)
2012	40	$67,500	8.0%	(3)
2013	41	$71,000	5.2%	(3)
2014	42	$73,500	3.5%	(3)
2015	43	$76,000	3.4%	(3)
2016	44	$78,000	2.6%	(3)
2017	45	$85,000	9.0%	(3)
2018	Deceased	$0	-100.0%	Deceased

Average Income Growth Rate (2014 to 2016): 5.00%

Job Information:

(1) Attending Graduate School, University of Nita
(2) Computer Instructor, Nita City Unified School District
(3) Computer Instructor, Techno-Soft, Inc.

POTTER V. SHRACKLE AND THE SHRACKLE CONSTRUCTION COMPANY REBUTTAL DAMAGES MODEL OF ELIZABETH C. BUCHANAN, PhD

TABLE 4. FUTURE VALUE OF FRINGE BENEFITS OF KATHERINE POTTER, AGE 45 TO 60

Date of Birth:	June 15, 1972
Date of Death:	December 4, 2017
Appraisal Period:	2019 to 2031
Projected Retirement Age:	55
Discount Rate:	6.00%
Benefits as % of Income:	17.50%

Year	Projected Age	Projected Value of Fringe Benefits	Present Discounted Value of Fringe Benefits
2017	45	$14,875	
2018	46	$15,619	$15,619
2019	47	$16,400	$16,400
2020	48	$17,221	$16,246
2021	49	$18,082	$16,093
2022	50	$18,987	$15,942
2023	51	$9,968	$7,896
2024	52	$10,467	$7,822
2025	53	$10,991	$7,748
2026	54	$11,540	$7,675
2027	55	$12,118	$7,603
2028	56	(RETIRED)	(RETIRED)
2029	51	(RETIRED)	(RETIRED)
2030	58	(RETIRED)	(RETIRED)
2031	59	(RETIRED)	(RETIRED)
2032	60	(RETIRED)	(RETIRED)
Value of Future Fringe Benefits:		$141,394	$119,044

POTTER V. SHRACKLE AND THE SHRACKLE CONSTRUCTION COMPANY REBUTTAL DAMAGES MODEL OF ELIZABETH C. BUCHANAN, PhD

TABLE 5. FUTURE VALUE OF HOUSEHOLD WORK OF KATHERINE POTTER, AGE 45 TO 60

Date of Birth:	June 15, 1972		
Date of Death:	December 4, 2017		
Appraisal Period:	2019 to 2031		
Projected Retirement Age:	55		
Discount Rate:	6.00%		
		Before Retirement	During Retirement
# of Hours Per Day at Household Work:		2	4
Days Per Year Doing Household Work:		250	250
Total Hours Per Year:		500	1,000

Year	Projected Age	Hourly Replacement Wage for Household Work	Projected Value of Household Work	Present Discounted Value of Household Work	
2017	45	$6.00	$3,000		
2018	46	$6.00	$3,000	$3,000	
2019	47	$6.00	$3,000	$3,000	
2020	48	$6.00	$3,000	$2,830	
2021	49	$6.00	$3,000	$2,670	
2022	50	$6.50	$3,250	$2,729	
2023	51	$6.50	$3,250	$2,574	
2024	52	$6.50	$3,250	$2,429	
2025	53	$6.50	$3,250	$2,291	
2026	54	$7.00	$3,500	$2,328	
2027	55	$7.00	$3,500	$2,196	
2028	56	$7.00	$7,000	$4,143	(RETIRED)
2029	57	$7.00	$7,000	$3,909	(RETIRED)
2030	58	$7.50	$7,500	$3,951	(RETIRED)
2031	59	$7.50	$7,500	$3,727	(RETIRED)
2032	60	$7.50	$7,500	$3,516	(RETIRED)
Value of Future Household Work:			$68,500	$45,293	

TABLE 6. FUTURE VALUE OF PERSONAL CONSUMPTION OF KATHERINE POTTER, AGE 45 TO 60

Date of Birth:	June 15, 1972
Date of Death:	December 4, 2017
Appraisal Period:	2019 to 2031
Projected Retirement Age:	55
Discount Rate:	6.00%
Consumption as % of Full-Time Income:	75.10%

Year	Projected Age	Projected Value of Personal Consumption	Present Discounted Value of Personal Consumption
2017	45	$63,835	
2018	46	$67,028	$67,028
2019	47	$70,381	$70,381
2020	48	$73,902	$69,719
2021	49	$77,599	$69,063
2022	50	$81,481	$68,413
2023	51	$42,778	$33,885
2024	52	$44,918	$33,566
2025	53	$47,165	$33,250
2026	54	$49,525	$32,937
2027	55	$52,002	$32,627
2028	56	(RETIRED)	(RETIRED)
2029	57	(RETIRED)	(RETIRED)
2030	58	(RETIRED)	(RETIRED)
2031	59	(RETIRED)	(RETIRED)
2032	60	(RETIRED)	(RETIRED)
Value of Future Consumption:		$606,781	$510,868

Dr. Elizabeth C. Buchanan

Business Address:
Department of Economics, DB #234
Nita State University, CB# 233
Nita City, Nita
(555) 555-4387
Fax: (555) 555-4388
Email: ebuchan@email.nsu.edu

Education:

BS University of Nita, 2003 (economics); PhD University of Nita, 2007 (economics)

Current Position:

Assistant Professor of Economics, Nita State University. Concentration in labor economics and industrial organization.

Employment History:

Assistant Professor of Economics, Nita State University since 2012. Dunhill Consultants, private economics consulting group, 2007–2012.

Principal Publications since 2007:

"The Value of Household Services," 18 *Journal of Labor Economics* 284 (2009)

"Damage Assessment for the Infringement of Intellectual Property Rights," 82 *Contemporary Economics Problems* 1204 (2013)

"Economic Loss in Copyright Cases," 4 *Journal of Law and Economics* 48 (2014)

"Can We Accurately Evaluate Lost Wages?" 7 *Journal of Law and Economics* 87 (2017)

"Intellectual Property and Modern Economic Thought," 80 *Harvard Public Policy Review* 438 (2019)

Expert Testimony:

Homer v. Underhill, Nita Superior Court, June 2012 (personal injury case, testified for the plaintiff with regard to economic loss resulting from injury)

Glandon v. Schwartz, Nita Superior Court, May 2014 (wrongful death case, testified for defendant with regard to economic loss resulting from death)

Marydale v. Farrer, Nita Superior Court, September 2017 (personal injury case, testified for the defendant with regard to economic loss resulting from injury)

MEMORANDUM

To: Robert Glenn, PhD

From: Steve Dyer, Research Assistant

Date: September 16, 2019

Re: Potter v. Shrackle

CONFIDENTIAL

Per your request, I've read through Dr. Buchanan's expert report in the Potter case. Contrasting her analysis with yours, I think the following points are important.

First, Dr. Buchanan assumes that Katherine Potter will completely stop working at age fifty-five. In his deposition, Daniel Sloan, her boss, stated that "She told me that there was no way that she would retire before she was sixty." Dr. Buchanan doesn't address this testimony in her expert report. In fact, the deposition testimony of Jeffrey Potter indicates that, although he mentioned early retirement to her, Ms. Potter did not agree to it.

Second, Dr. Buchanan does not include the possibility that Ms. Potter might have been promoted, which would have resulted in an increase in Ms. Potter's annual salary. Mr. Sloan mentioned in his deposition that his "business is expanding" and "Ms. Potter was exactly the kind of person" the business needed because "she had all of the technical skills as well as an extraordinary ability to work with people." Mr. Sloan even goes as far as saying that he "was grooming her to become an executive vice-president." This indicates that it is very likely that Ms. Potter would have been promoted before she retired and would have received a commensurate boost in her salary. Dr. Buchanan assumes that she wouldn't be promoted and her salary growth would be stagnant.

Third, Dr. Buchanan understates the value of Ms. Potter's fringe benefits as a percentage of her annual salary. She uses 17.5 percent of Ms. Potter's salary to calculate benefits. However, the actual amount of benefits, excluding the $10,000 bonus, is closer to 17.65 percent. Even though it is probably not a large difference in terms of damages, it is an inaccuracy in her report. More importantly, I believe your estimates using 20 percent for the fringe benefits package is correct. In his deposition, Daniel Sloan states, "At the time of her death, her fringe benefits package was 20 percent of her salary. This included contribution to a retirement plan, medical and dental insurance, as well as life and disability insurance." Based upon this statement, the $10,000 bonus is not included in the 20 percent which Mr. Sloan talks about. I think Dr. Buchanan was confused when she talked to Linda Graham and thought the $10,000 was included in Mr. Sloan's 20 percent figure for fringe benefits.

Fourth, Dr. Buchanan uses minimum wage as the replacement cost for the loss of Ms. Potter's household labor. Some household chores, however, should be valued at more than the minimum wage, such as cooking and gardening, as Mr. Potter really could not find somebody to do such things for minimum wage. In addition, to the extent that Ms. Potter had specialized skills (such as managing the household finances, preparing tax returns, etc.), the value of her lost work should be valued at its replacement cost, which would likely be higher than minimum wage.

On the other hand, I note in your report that you use Ms. Potter's imputed hourly wage at Techno-Soft, Inc. to value her lost household work. I think the calculation comes out to be somewhere around $41 per hour for her imputed wage. Even if Dr. Buchanan underestimates the value of Ms. Potter's lost household work using the hourly minimum wage, I think using her imputed Techno-Soft, Inc. wage may overstate the value of her lost household work insofar as it would not take someone making $41 per hour to do basic, unskilled household work.

Fifth, both you and Dr. Buchanan use the same discount rate in your calculations.

Sixth, both you and Dr. Buchanan use the same consumption rate in your calculations.

I will continue to look for more documents that can better support our arguments. In the meantime, I will come by your office later in the week so that you can approve my time sheet.

Exhibits Available to Both Sides

Exhibit 1

Department of Transportation
Bureau of Safety
Programing and Analysis
T&S Building, Nita City, Nita

NITA POLICE DEPARTMENT TRAFFIC ACCIDENT REPORT

Page 1 of 2

Investigating Officer/ Badge No.	Michael Young / #7319	Date of Report: 12/4/17	Approved By/ Date

Date	11/30/17	Time 3:28	County Darrow	City Nita City

No. Vehicles 1	No. Killed 1	No. Injuried	Municipality

Principal Road

Street Name: Mattis   Speed Limit:

Nearest Cross Street: Kirby   Check if One Way: ☐ N ☐ S ☐ E ☐ W

Intersecting Road

Street Name: Speed Limit:

Direction From Accident Site: ☐ N ☐ S ☐ E ☐ W

Illumination	Weather	Road Surface	Traffic Control Device Type	
☐ Dawn or Dusk	☒ No Adverse Conditions	☒ Dry	☐ No Controls	☐ RR Crossing Controls
☒ Daylight	☐ Raining	☐ Wet	☐ Flashing Traffic Signal	☐ Police Officer/Flagman
☐ Dark (with street lights)	☐ Sleet/Hail	☐ Muddy	☒ Traffic Signal	☐ Flashing School Zone Sign
☐ Dark (with no street lights)	☐ Snowing	☐ Snow/Ice	☐ Stop Sign	☐ Other
	☐ Fog/Smoke		☐ Yield Sign	

Vehicle Driver No. 1

☒ Moving   ☐ Stopped in Traffic   ☐ Parked   ☐ Pedestrian   ☐ Bicyclist   ☐ Other

Drivers Name (First, Middle, Last)	Charles T. Shrackle	Divers License Number	State
Street Address	1701 W Johnston	Date of Birth 5/13/73	
City Nita City	State Nita Zip Code	Telephone Numbers	
Vehicle (Year/Make) 2001 Toyota pickup	License Plate or ID Number	State Nita	
Vehicle Owner	Charles T. Shrackle	Date of Birth	
Address	City	State	Zip Code

Vehicle Driver No. 2

☐ Moving   ☐ Stopped in Traffic   ☐ Parked   ☒ Pedestrian   ☐ Bicyclist   ☐ Other

Drivers Name (First, Middle, Last)	Katherine Potter	Divers License Number	State
Street Address	4920 Thorndale Avenue	Date of Birth	
City Nita City	State Nita Zip Code	Telephone Numbers	
Vehicle (Year/Make)	License Plate or ID Number	State	
Vehicle Owner		Date of Birth	
Address	City	State	Zip Code

Exhibit 1 (cont'd)

Department of Transportation
Bureau of Safety
Programing and Analysis
T&S Building, Nita City, Nita

NITA POLICE DEPARTMENT TRAFFIC ACCIDENT REPORT

Page 2 of 2

Witnesses

(A) Juanita and Vicky Williams
    1010 W Kirby #15
    Nita

(B) Marilyn Kelly
    1910 Elden Lane
    Nita

Narrative

#1 was southbound on Mattis after turning left from Kirby. He then struck #2 (pedestrian) approx 30 feet S of pedestrian crosswalk. #1 said he didn't see pedestrian until after he struck her. Witnesses A (mother & daughter) had been in car driving east on Kirby and saw pedestrian running across street westbound. Neither saw actual contact.

On 12/1/17 witness B called station and said pedestrian was in crosswalk.

On 12/4/17 I was informed that pedestrian had died.

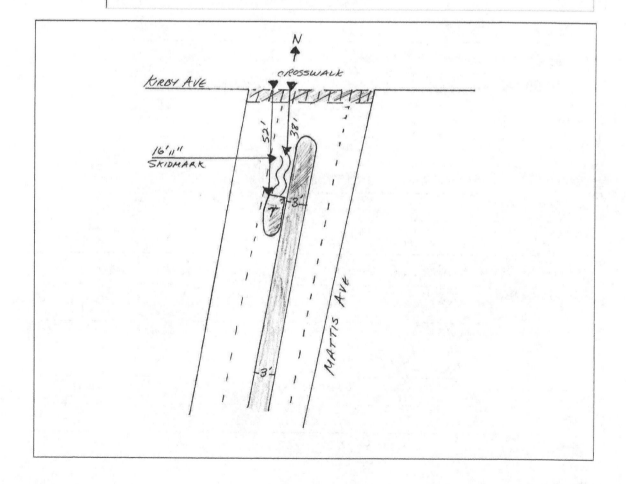

Exhibit 2

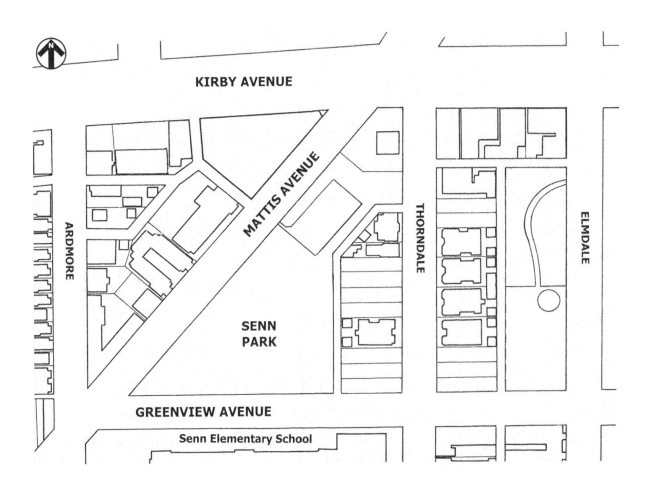

Exhibit 2a

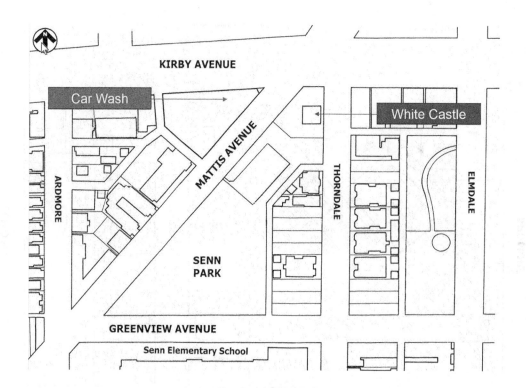

Exhibit 2b

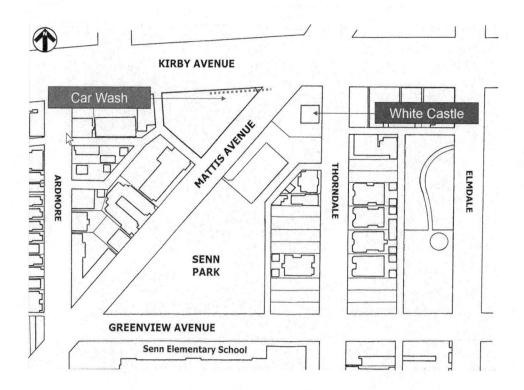

Exhibit 2c

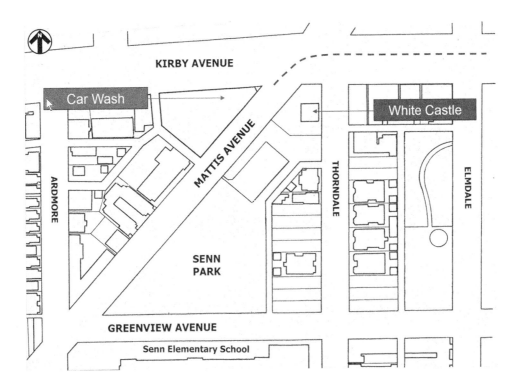

Exhibit 2d

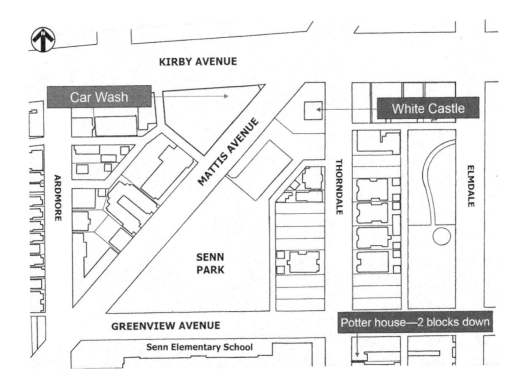

Exhibit 3

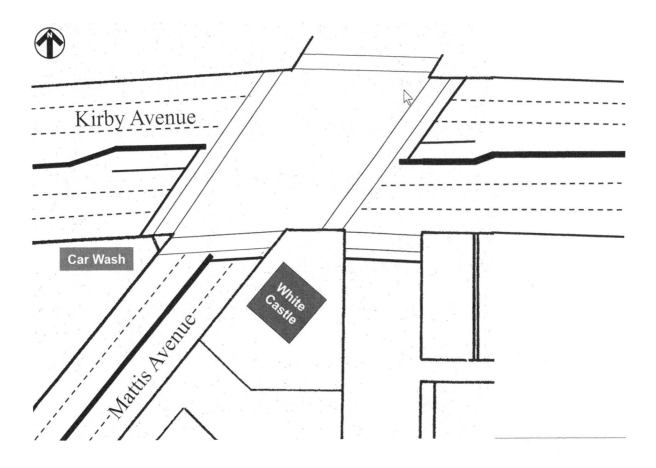

Exhibit 3a

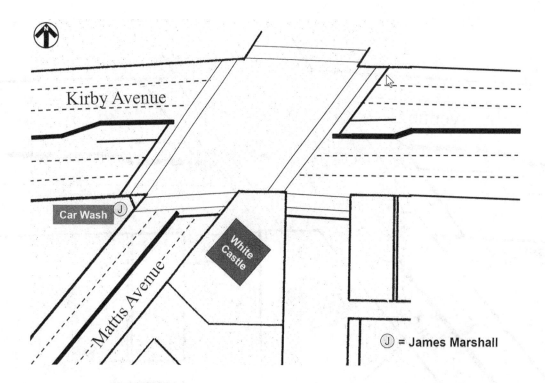

Exhibit 3b

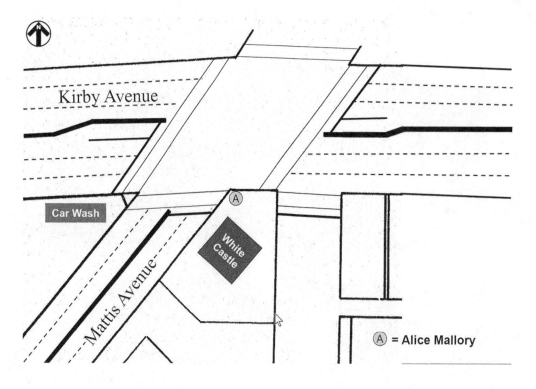

Exhibit 3c

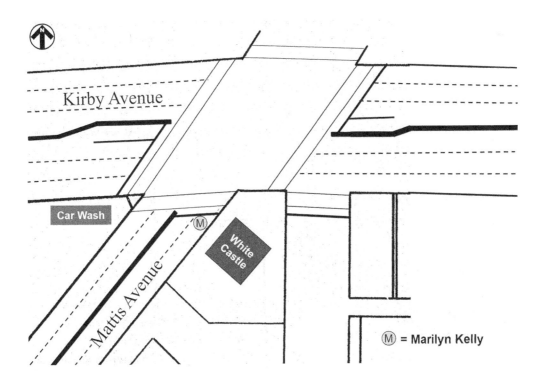

Exhibit 3d

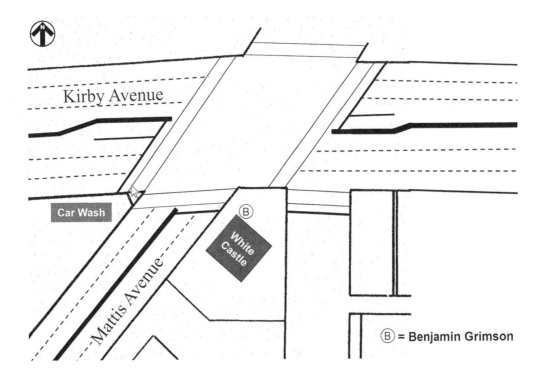

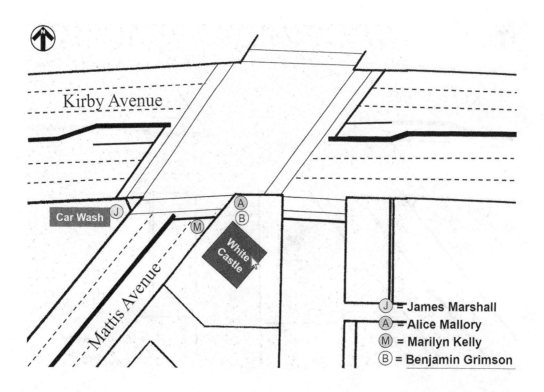

Exhibit 4

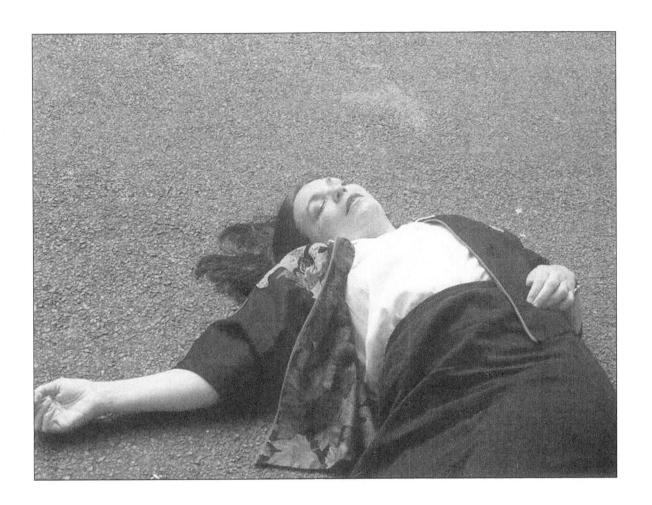

Exhibit 5

Exhibit 6

Exhibit 7

Exhibit 8

Exhibit 9

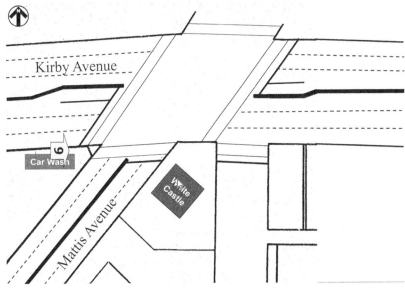

Exhibit 10

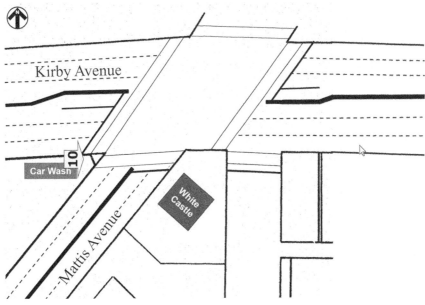

Exhibit 11

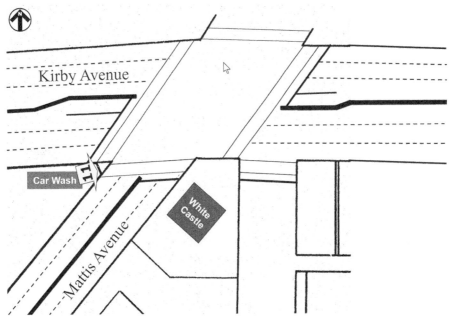

Exhibit 12

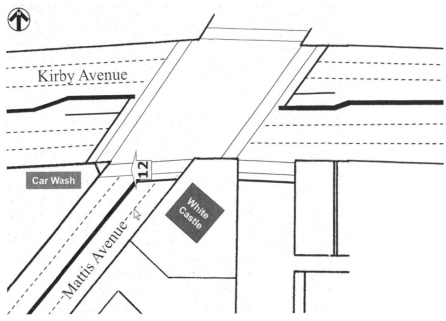

Exhibit 13

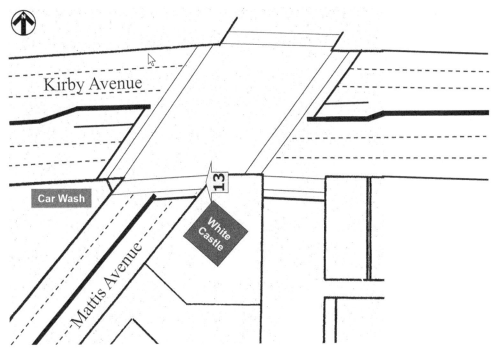

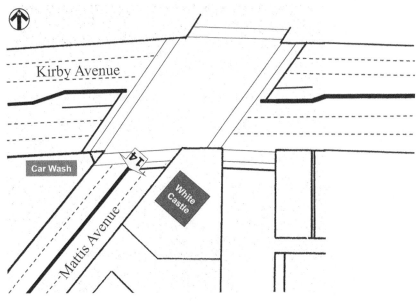

Exhibit 15

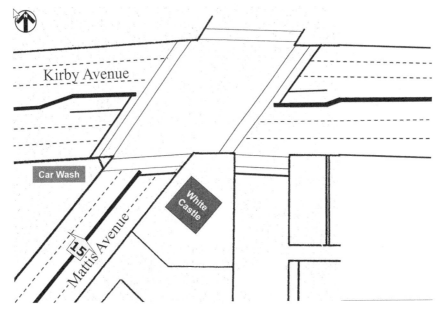

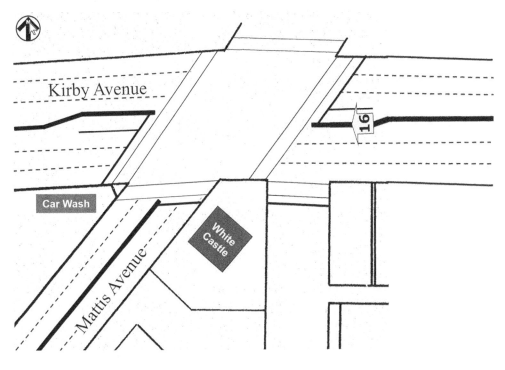

Exhibit 17

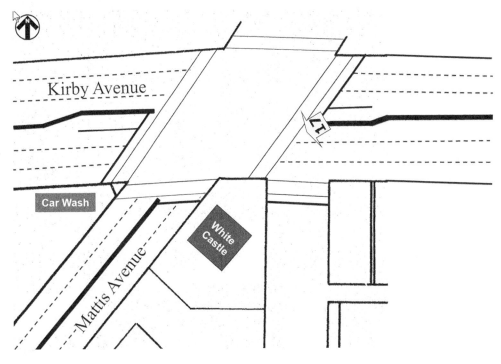

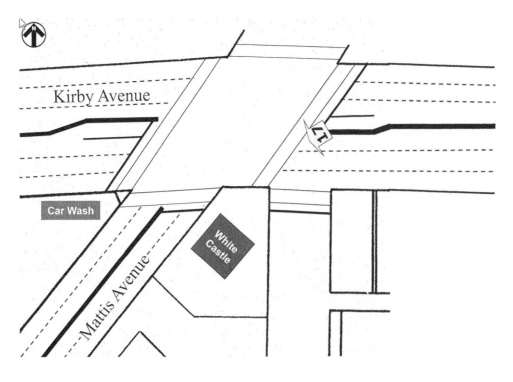

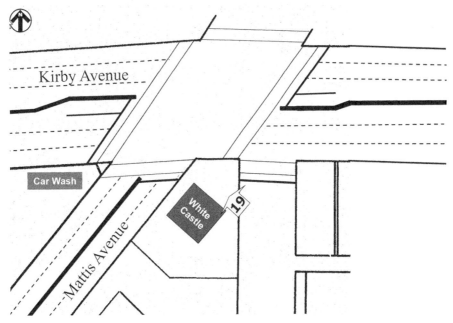

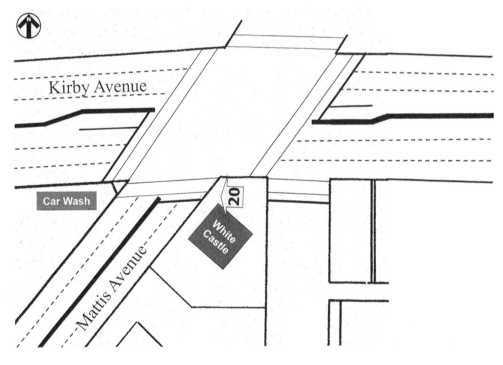

Exhibit 21

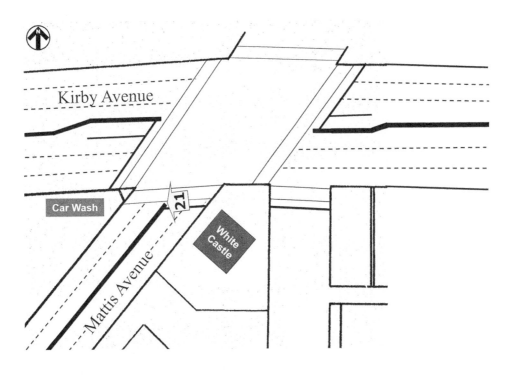

Exhibit 22*

Statement of James Marshall

I am the owner-operator of Jim Marshall's
tires, 1601 (~~1610~~) Kirby, Nita City, Nita. I was
working in the car wash portion of my
business on Nov. 30, 2017.

At approximately 3:30 on Nov. 30, 2017,
I was doing some maintenance work on
one of the vacuum units for the car wash.
It was the second (~~first~~) from the corner. I saw
a dark-haired woman walking east on the
south sidewalk of Kirby. When I saw her,
she was 15 or 20 feet from the intersection.
I looked over at my employee, Ed Putnam,
to ask him something about the job we
were doing. About a minute or minute
and a half later I heard a thump.
I looked out and saw a pickup truck
carrying a body on the front of it.
I sent Putnam out to see if he could
be of help while I called the police.
I went out to see if I could be of
help and saw the same woman that
I'd seen earlier walking east on
Kirby lying on the pavement.

Signed: James Marshall
Witness: Joseph Lucey
Dec. 12, 2017

---

* Marshall's business is located on the southwest corner of Kirby and Mattis. This statement was taken by Joseph Lucey, an adjuster for the defendant's insurance carrier, on December 8, 2017, at about 11 a.m. The statement was written by Mr. Lucey. The signature and the correction are in Marshall's handwriting.

Exhibit 23

Clark Poe

From: Clark Poe <cpoe@poecon.nita>
Sent: Monday, November 24, 2017 9:34 AM
To: Charles Shrackle
Subject: Greenbriar

Charlie: The delays on the Greenbriar project are unacceptable. We are so far behind that the developer, Mr. Green, is about ready to cancel the job and get a new contractor. Legally, he can probably do it.

I know that you've had some trouble with rock, but there is always trouble with rock in this area. We need to finish this job immediately!

Come to the job site at 3:30 p.m. tomorrow and be ready to give me a detailed description of your problems and a firm commitment on a conclusion date. This has become a real problem, Charlie, so be there and be on time.

Clark
Clark Poe Construction Company
414 Whitebread Road
Nita City, Nita 99992
(555) 828-1891
cpoe@poecon.nita

Exhibit 24

Charles T. Shrackle

From: Charles T. Shrackle <cts@shrackleconstruction.nita>
Sent: Monday, November 24, 2017 10:23 AM
To: Clark Poe (cpoe@poecon.nita)
Subject: Greenbriar

Clark: I hear you loud and clear. I'll be there at 3:30 tomorrow. Unlike sometimes in the past, I assure you I won't be late.

Charlie

Charles T. Shrackle
Shrackle Construction Company
Route 45
Sommers Township
Nita City, Nita 99994
(555) 826-9406

Exhibit 25

Nita City Weather Channel
www.ncweather.nita

Weather report for Nita City, Nita on November 30, 2017

Sunny
56°
Chance of Rain: 0%
Wind: W at 11 mph
Sunny skies. High 56F. Winds W at 10 to 15 mph.

Sunrise: 6:55 am	**Sunset:** 4:21 pm

Exhibit 26

NMH Nita Memorial Hospital

444 Medway Park Circle Nita City, Nita 40088 (555)555-4444

SF-1 Statement

Please note: This is a short form statement listing general charges, Itemization statements are available upon request for all services and goods provided.

Statement date:	12/7/17
Patient:	Katherine Potter (deceased)
Patient ID:	4478-622-00
Admitted:	Yes
Time/date of initial treatment:	4:18 p.m., 11/30/17
ER attending physician:	Ashley P. Smith, MD, #609
Other physician(s):	Kevin M. Patterson, MD #711
Brief description:	Severe head trauma, brain injury, and fractured skull; result of being struck by moving vehicle. Intermittent consciousness; surgery to relieve pressure on brain.
Release date:	T O D 12/4/2017, 4:00 p.m.

11/30/17	NMH ambulance service	$840
11/30/17	Emergency room	$4,500
	ER physician (Ref: Ashley P. Smith, MD, #609)	$4,080
	Medications administered	$1,660
11/30/17–12/4/17	Intensive care private room and attendant care 5 days $17,000	$84,200
12/1/17	Physician, surgery, medications; tests; blood, IV	$11,720
12/4/17	NMH morgue service	$800
	Total	$107,800

This statement is for general billing information only and not intended for insurance submission. Insurance claims may be pending and are not necessarily reflected on this statement. Itemizations of all charges are available on request.

Exhibit 27

Odell Funeral Home

2002 Eternity Way, Nita City, Nita

(555) 555-7734

Confidential Invoice

INVOICE DATE   January 12, 2018

SERVICES FOR: Katherine Potter, December 11, 2017

20-gauge reinforced "Norabella" casket, sealed	$ 8,000
Heavy duty gasket, screw lock, seal kit	229
Delivery included	
General prep services	600
Additional prep	200
Silk flower casket spray (blue, white, gold)	200
Memorial stone	2,300
Photo etched	375
"Restful Garden" Mausoleum, unit 40	3,000
Peace Garden Cemetery, Nita City, service fee	980
Limousine 2 hours @ 270.50/hour	541
10-inch obituary in Nita Journal-Gazette with photo	75
TOTAL DUE, NET 30:	$16,500.00

Established 1924

Exhibit 28

4920 Thorndale Avenue
Nita City, Nita 99993
September 2, 2017

Dr. Andrew Stevens
Stevens Counseling
1225 North Street
Lisle, Nita 99980

Dear Dr. Stevens:

I am sorry that payment for our last three sessions is late. I guess it goes without saying that Katherine and I don't see eye to eye on the need for this counseling, and it is very difficult for me to get her to even speak calmly about it, much less agree for us to pay for it. Nonetheless,

I am enclosing our check in the amount of $300.

I am sorry that we can't continue with you. I thought your advice was very helpful and I appreciated the opportunity to talk with you about the problems that we have been having. I especially want to thank you for your concern about the early retirement issue. Even though Katherine loves her career, I am confident she would like the leisurely life of a college professor's wife even more. When we first got married, I was unable to talk her into having children. She was too career-driven. I hope that I can make more headway on the retirement issue.

Your comments at the last session that it was obvious to you that Katherine and I loved each other very much, and would come out of this stronger than ever, make me smile and look forward to the future. I am sure that you are right. Perhaps when we have more time and her career isn't so hectic, I'll be able to persuade Katherine to come back with me to talk to you about the rest of our problems, which don't seem quite so important now. Despite all the difficulties, I believe that our marriage will work. If it doesn't, so be it. If we can't resolve things, I can leave the marriage and seek a relationship that fulfills my needs.

In any event, keep your fingers crossed for us, please. Sincerely yours,

Jeffrey T. Potter

Jeffrey T. Potter

Exhibit 29

Madden & James

Suite 720 • Nita Bank Building • Nita City, Nita 99994 • (555) 555-0003

James Barber
Pierce, Johnson & Clark
Nita National Bank Plaza
Nita City, Nita 99994

September 18, 2019

Re: *Potter v. Shrackle and Shrackle Construction Co.*

Jim:

Although I think there is no obligation to do this under the Rules, I thought I would update Jeffrey Potter's answers at his deposition with regard to his relationship with Cheryl Tobias. If asked about that relationship at this point, Mr. Potter would state:

I began a relationship with Cheryl Tobias in the late spring of 2018. That relationship ended in December 2018. The basis for ending the relationship was that I was unable to move on to another long-term relationship after the death of my wife. Cheryl and I agreed it would be better to break off the relationship at that point.

I would be happy to sign a request to admit to this effect.

Sincerely,

William James

William James

Exhibit 30

PRIMARY OPEN-ANGLE GLAUCOMA

Open-angle glaucoma is the most common form of glaucoma. It is also known as "primary" or "chronic" glaucoma and accounts for at least ninety percent of all glaucoma cases. "Open-angle" is used to denote that the angle where the iris meets the cornea is as open and wide as it should be. This condition affects about three million Americans and occurs mainly in people over fifty.

There are no noticeable symptoms with primary open-angle glaucoma. The eye's intraocular pressure (IOP) slowly increases and the cornea adapts without swelling. The IOP increases either when too much aqueous humor fluid (transparent, watery fluid containing low protein concentrations) is produced or by a decrease in aqueous humor outflow. The trabecular meshwork (tissue located around the base of the cornea) is responsible for most of the outflow of aqueous humor. Swelling is an indicator that something is wrong; without it, the disease often goes undetected. Patients do not feel pain and often do not realize there is an issue until the later stages of the disease and a loss of vision.

The increased pressure in the eye ultimately destroys optic nerve cells. Once enough of the nerve cells are destroyed, blind spots begin to form in the patient's field of vision. The blind spots usually start in the peripheral (outer areas) field of vision. As the disease progresses, the central vision also becomes affected. Once the vision is impaired, the damage is irreversible. There is currently no treatment to restore the dead nerve cells.

Primary open-angle glaucoma is a chronic disease. There is currently no cure for it, but the disease can be slowed through treatment. There are medications, when taken regularly, that can be crucial to preventing further damage to a patient's vision. Eye drops generally are the initial treatment as they can reduce IOP by decreasing aqueous production or increasing aqueous outflow. If the patient does not respond to medication, then surgery will be indicated.

There is no visible abnormality of the trabecular meshwork. It is believed that the ability of the cells in the trabecular meshwork to carry out their normal function is compromised. It is also possible that there may be fewer cells in the meshwork as a natural result of getting older. Others believe it is because of a structural defect in the eye's drainage system or that the condition is caused by an enzymatic problem. All of these theories are currently being studied at various research centers.

NMJ NITA Medical Journal MAY 2017

Exhibit 31

Exhibit 32

Exhibit 33

Billing period Nov 12, 2017 to Dec 11, 2017| Account # 1111101-00001 | Invoice # 123456789

Charles T. Shrackle
555.123.4567 | Nita City

Talk activity - continued

Date	Time	Number	Origination	Destination	Min.	Airtime Charges
Nov 25	3:23 PM	555.749.3112	Nita City, NITA	Nita City, NITA	1	--
Nov 26	3:31 PM	555.749.3112	Nita City, NITA	Nita City, NITA	31	--
Nov 27	12:26 PM	800.234.7350	Nita City, NITA	Nita City, NITA	7	--
Nov 29	1:31 PM	555.537.3232	Nita City, NITA	Incoming, NITA	22	--
Nov 30	10:29 AM	800.546.7800	Nita City, NITA	Toll-Free, NITA	22	--
Nov 30	10:50 AM	800.546.7800	Nita City, NITA	Toll-Free, NITA	1	--
Nov 30	10:51 AM	800.546.7800	Nita City, NITA	Toll-Free, NITA	13	--
Nov 30	12:25 PM	800.546.7800	Nita City, NITA	Toll-Free, NITA	49	--
Nov 30	2:58 PM	555.474.5612	Nita City, NITA	Nita City, NITA	1	--
Nov 30	3:24 PM	555.353.6600	Nita City, NITA	Nita City, NITA	2	--
Nov 30	11:40 AM	800.906.9330	Nita City, NITA	Toll-Free, NITA	12	--
Dec 1	2:26 PM	555.400.4453	Nita City, NITA	Nita City, NITA	2	--
Dec 2	4:30 PM	800.234.7350	Nita City, NITA	Toll-Free, NITA	11	--
Dec 3	4:48 PM	555.400.4453	Nita City, NITA	Incoming, NITA	31	--
Dec 4	7:22 AM	800.424.2449	Nita City, NITA	Toll-Free, NITA	11	--
Dec 5	9:52 AM	555.227.4786	Nita City, NITA	Nita City, NITA	1	--
Dec 6	11:40 AM	555.474.5612	Nita City, NITA	Nita City, NITA	14	--
Dec 7	10:28 AM	555.474.5612	Nita City, NITA	Incoming, NITA	9	--
Dec 7	5:31 PM	555.493.0494	Nita City, NITA	Nita City, NITA	1	--

Exhibits Available to Defendant's Law Firm

Exhibit 34

NITA TRAVEL COMPANY

eTICKET RECEIPT

Reservation Code:	WQMFKA	Issuing Agent:	Nita City, Nita
Ticket Number:	8675309502425	Issuing Agent:	3BA78/4076
Issuing Airline:	CARIBBEAN AIRLINES	IATA number:	66397478
Date Issued:	30May18	Invoice number:	483228
Customer Number:	8972509574		
Passenger:	Jeffrey Potter		

14JUN18   Caribbean Air CA 1066   Seat 15B

From: Nita City, Nita (Nita City Intern'l)   Departs: 730A   Business Confirmed

To: Fort de France, Martinique (FDF)   Arrives: 355P   Fare Basis: TC8BX

Not Valid Before: 14JUN

Not Valid After: 14JUN

19JUN18   Caribbean Air CA 3631

From: Fort de France, Martinique (FDF)   Departs: 1150A   Business Confirmed

To: Nita City, Nita (Nita City Intern'l)   Arrives: 820P   Fare Basis: TC8BX

Not Valid Before: 19JUN

Not Valid After: 19JUN

Form of Payment: Credit Card - Visa - Charged to Jeffrey Potter

Endorsement/Restrictions: Nonref/Change Fee Plus Fare Diff Applies/Valid US Only

Positive Identification Required for Airport Check-In

Carriage and other service provided by the carrier are subject to conditions of carriage, which are hereby incorporated by reference. These conditions may be obtained from the issuing carrier.

Nita Travel Company . . . Your Gateway to Fun in the Sun!

Exhibit 35

NITA TRAVEL COMPANY   eTICKET RECEIPT

Reservation Code:	WQMFKA	Issuing Agent:	Nita City, Nita
Ticket Number:	5996739313271	Issuing Agent:	3BA78/4076
Issuing Airline:	CARIBBEAN AIRLINES	IATA number:	66397478
Date Issued:	30May18	Invoice number:	483228
Customer Number:	2896768575		
Passenger:	Cheryl Tobias		

14JUN18 Caribbean Air CA 1066	Seat 15A	
From: Nita City, Nita (Nita City Intern'l)	Departs: 730A	Business Confirmed
To: Fort de France, Martinique (FDF)	Arrives: 355P	Fare Basis: TC8BX
		Not Valid Before: 14JUN
		Not Valid After: 14JUN
19JUN18 Caribbean Air CA 3631		
From: Fort de France, Martinique (FDF)	Departs: 1150A	Business Confirmed
To: Nita City, Nita (Nita City Intern'l)	Arrives: 820P	Fare Basis: TC8BX
		Not Valid Before: 19JUN
		Not Valid After: 19JUN

Form of Payment: Credit Card - Visa - Charged to Jeffrey Potter

Endorsement/Restrictions: Nonref/Change Fee Plus Fare Diff Applies/Valid US Only

Positive Identification Required for Airport Check-In

Carriage and other service provided by the carrier are subject to conditions of carriage, which are hereby incorporated by reference. These conditions may be obtained from the issuing carrier.

Nita Travel Company . . . Your Gateway to Fun in the Sun!

Exhibit 36

Martinique Princess Hotel
76 Rue de la Plage
Forte de France, Martinique

Name: Mr. & Mrs. Jeffrey Potter   Guests: 2
Address: 4920 Thorndale Avenue   Room: 1370
          Nita City, Nita

Arrival: 6/14/18   Departure: 6/19/18

Date	Description	ID	Ref. No.	Charges	Credits Balance
6/14/18	Room/Deluxe Suite	MRC	1370	325.00	
6/14/18	I. Room Tax	MIT	1370	29.65	
6/14/18	City Occup. Tax	MOE	1370	10.98	
6/14/18	Room Service	MCH	1370	48.19	
6/15/18	Room/Deluxe Suite	MRC	1370	325.00	
6/15/18	I. Room Tax	MIT	1370	29.65	
6/15/18	City Occup. Tax	MOE	1370	10.98	
6/15/18	Masseuse	MAS	1370	80.50	
6/15/18	Masseuse	MAS	1370	80.50	
6/15/18	Room Service	MCH	1370	28.99	
6/15/18	Room Service	MCH	1370	158.90	
6/16/18	Room/Deluxe Suite	MRC	1370	325.00	
6/16/18	I. Room Tax	MIT	1370	29.65	
6/16/18	City Occup. Tax	MOE	1370	10.98	
6/16/18	Day Spa	MSG	1370	125.29	
6/16/18	Day Spa	MSG	1370	60.13	
6/16/18	Room Service	MCH	1370	33.48	
6/16/18	Laundry Services	MLS	1370	71.17	
6/16/18	Boutique	MBB	1370	148.75	
6/16/18	Room Service	MCH	1370	48.30	
6/16/18	Champagne Cruise	MCC	1370	198.45	
6/16/18	Champagne Cruise	MCC	1370	198.45	
6/17/18	Room/Deluxe Suite	MRC	1370	325.00	
6/17/18	I. Room Tax	MIT	1370	29.65	
6/17/18	City Occup. Tax	MOE	1370	10.98	

Exhibit 36 (cont'd)

Date	Description	ID	Ref. No.	Charges	Credits Balance
6/17/18	Room Service	MCH	1370	68.90	
6/17/18	Tarot Card Reader	MTR	1370	51.50	
6/17/18	Masseuse	MAS	1370	80.50	
6/17/18	Room Service	MCH	1370	62.99	
6/17/18	Day Spa	MSG	1370	75.22	
6/17/18	Flower Show	MFB	1370	31.00	
6/17/18	Room Service	MCH	1370	79.42	
6/17/18	Room Service	MCH	1370	108.14	
6/17/18	Movies	MOV	1370	15.00	
6/18/18	Room/Deluxe Suite	MRC	1370	325.00	
6/18/18	I. Room Tax	MIT	1370	29.65	
6/18/18	City Occup. Tax	MOE	1370	10.98	
6/18/18	Day Spa	MSG	1370	28.68	
6/18/18	Room Service	MCH	1370	43.10	
6/18/18	Island Tour	MCL	1370	58.33	
6/18/18	Island Tour	MCL	1370	58.33	
6/18/18	Room Service	MCH	1370	61.30	
6/18/18	Champagne Cruise	MCC	1370	198.45	
6/18/18	Champagne Cruise	MCC	1370	198.45	
6/19/18	Room Service	MCH	1370	38.95	

$4,304.52

I agree that my liability for this bill is not waived and agree to be held personally liable in the event that the indicated person, company, or association fails to pay for any part or the full amount of these charges.

Thank you for being our guest at the Martinique Princess Hotel.

Exhibit 37

DUDLEY INVESTIGATIONS
765 NITA AVENUE
NITA CITY, NITA 99994

Memo to File: Potter v. Shrackle

Dated: July 15, 2019

Re: Vehicle driven by witness Juanita Williams
and Shrackle Phone Record

cc: James Barber
Pierce, Johnson & Clark
Nita National Bank Plaza
Nita City, Nita 99994

The three attached photos are of the front end, back end, and view out the back from the back seat of a 2015 Toyota Highlander, which is the same make, model, and year as the vehicle driven by witness Juanita Williams on November 30, 2017.

I also contacted the client and asked for his cell phone record for November 2017, which he provided and is attached.

S. Dudley, Investigator

Exhibit 37a

Exhibit 37b

Exhibit 37c

Exhibit 38

DUDLEY INVESTIGATIONS
765 NITA AVENUE
NITA CITY, NITA 99994

Memo to File: Potter v. Shrackle

Dated: August 15, 2019

Re: Mr. Potter's relationship with Cheryl Tobias

cc: James Barber
Pierce, Johnson & Clark
Nita National Bank Plaza
Nita City, Nita 99994

As part of my investigation, I went to the campus of the University of Nita to see what I might find out about plaintiff, Professor Jeffrey Potter. In talking to people around the Physics Department, I discovered there might be more to the relationship between Professor Potter and Graduate Student Cheryl Tobias than meets the eye. A close friend of Ms. Tobias, who asked to remain anonymous, told me she was upset with how this professor used his superior position at the University to engage in an improper sexual relationship with a female underling. She said she had counselled Ms. Tobias against entering into this relationship to no avail. When I asked her if she had proof of this relationship, she took out her smartphone and showed me several ImageGram postings she had received from her friend after a trip she took with Professor Potter to Martinique earlier this year. I explained who I was and what my role was in this litigation and asked if she would be willing to do a screen grab of these various postings and email them to me. She enthusiastically replied yes and sent me five ImageGram postings, which I have printed out and attached. I told her I would do everything I could to keep her and her identity out of this lawsuit.

_____

S. Dudley, Investigator

Exhibit 38a

Exhibit 38d

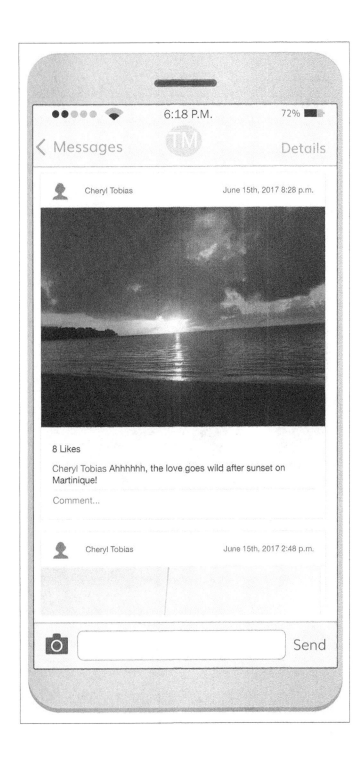

Exhibit 38e